Confessions
of a French Baker

Confessions
of a French Baker

BREADMAKING SECRETS,
TIPS, AND RECIPES

Peter Mayle

and Gerard Auzet

Alfred A. Knopf   New York   2005

THIS IS A BORZOI BOOK
PUBLISHED BY ALFRED A. KNOPF

www.aaknopf.com

Knopf, Borzoi Books, and the colophon are registered
trademarks of Random House, Inc.

Library of Congress Cataloging-in-Publication Data
Mayle, Peter.
Confessions of a French baker : breadmaking secrets,
tips, and recipes / Peter Mayle and Gerard Auzet.
p. cm.
ISBN 1-4000-4474-X (alk. paper)
1. Bread 2. Cookery, French—Provençal style. I. Auzet,
Gerard. II. Title.
TX769.M375 2005
641.8'15—dc22   2005045182

Manufactured in the United States of America
First Edition

To the artisan bakers of France,

who give us our daily bread

Contents

Introduction

"IN CAVAILLON, there are seventeen bakers listed in the *Pages Jaunes*, but we had been told that one establishment was ahead of all the rest in terms of choice and excellence, a veritable *palais de pain*. At Chez Auzet, so they said, the baking and eating of breads and pastries had been elevated to the status of a minor religion."

That was written in 1988, scribbled in one of the notebooks that were eventually turned into *A Year in Provence*. And ever since my first visit, the *boulangerie* Auzet has been one of my favorite places in Cavaillon.

It is not a mere shop, and certainly not somewhere for the hurried, in-and-out purchase. That would be to miss half the pleasure of going there, a pleasure that starts even before entering the premises. You pause for a moment on the threshold. You close your eyes, and, taking a long, deep breath (through the nose, of course), you inhale the *parfum de la maison*. Fresh, warm, buttery, doughy—it is one of the oldest, most appetizing and evocative smells in the world, primitive and infinitely comforting.

Gerard Auzet, who has taken over the business from Roger, his father, has become a friend. Whenever I go into the *boulangerie,* he greets me with a firm, floury handshake and a cup of coffee. Usually, we talk about bread. But one morning, he had more on his mind than the day's new batch of *croissants, boules,* and *fougasses.* He had a small but interesting problem.

Foreigners, many foreigners, had been coming to the bakery after reading about it, and it seemed they wanted more than bread. They also wanted knowledge: ingredients, recipes, tips—anything that might help them to bake their own bread *à la façon d'Auzet* when they returned home to San Francisco, Tokyo, Munich, London, or Amsterdam.

Gerard, being a generous and obliging man, started to give demonstrations for his overseas customers. Once a week, he would take a group of them into the baking room at the back of the shop and give them a two-hour class in bread making: how to shape the dough into *baguettes, boules,* and *bâtards,* how to decorate the dough with patterns of stripes and indentations, how to finish off the ends with satisfying blunt curves—and, finally, how to bake.

The demonstrations became more and more popular. But something was missing. Auzet's disciples, the students, kept asking for a reminder of their lesson to take home with them, a written reference, a kind of guide to basic baking.

"*Voilà le problème*," Gerard said to me. "Of course, they have my recipes. But I'd like to give them more than just a few sheets of paper. Perhaps some history, one or two anecdotes, a few hints—you know, a proper souvenir. A little book."

"I think that's a delightful idea," I said.

"Yes," said Gerard. "And you can write it for me."

And so I have, though the expertise is his.

—P.M., January 2005

Confessions
of a French Baker

The Birth of a Loaf

CAVAILLON, the melon capital of France (and of the world, according to the local melon fraternity), is a market town of some 23,000 inhabitants, about a thirty-minute drive from Avignon. By day, it's a lively, crowded place. Cars prowl the streets in search of a parking spot, housewives sniff and prod the glistening piles of fruit and vegetables laid out on sidewalk stands shaded by striped awnings, café regulars study newspapers over their morning beers as dogs sidle between the tables hoping to find a fallen *croissant*. The sounds of laughter, vigorous argument, and *les top hits* of Radio Vaucluse burst out through open doors and windows.

That was how I knew Cavaillon, and how I always thought of it, until I was invited to take a look behind the scenes of the Auzet bakery by the *patron* himself. It was to be a working visit. I wanted to see bakers in action. I wanted to witness mounds of dough being transformed into loaves. I wanted to run my fingers through the flour, squeeze a warm *boule* or two, and generally soak up the atmosphere.

That was no problem, Gerard Auzet told me. I could have the freedom of the bakery while it was still calm and uncrowded. He suggested that I turn up for work, like everyone else, at four a.m. He could guarantee I'd have no trouble parking.

Cavaillon at four on that August morning was cool and ghostly. There were no cars, no noise, no people, no hint of the heat that would come with the morning sun. I was aware of hearing sounds one seldom hears in a busy town: the ticking of my car's engine as it cooled, the wailing of a lovelorn cat, the click of my own footsteps. I walked past shuttered stores and groups of café chairs and tables that had been chained up on the pavement for the night. It felt strange to have the street to myself.

Gerard was waiting for me at the end of the Cours Bournissac, standing in a pool of light outside the entrance to his bakery. He was more cheerful than any man had a right to be at that time of the morning.

"We've already started," he said. "But you haven't missed much. Come on in."

It was still too early for the addict's fix, the warm and heavenly whiff of just-baked bread. That would come in an hour or so, filling the bakery, drifting out through the door, causing nostrils to twitch in anticipation. The very thought of it made me hungry.

For the first time, I saw the bakery in a state of undress, the shelves bare. By six a.m. those shelves would be filling up with loaves—tall and thick, long and slender, plump and round, plain and fancy, whole wheat, rye, bran, flavored with garlic or Roquefort cheese, studded with olives or walnuts—the twenty-one varieties that are baked and sold each day. (If none of these is exactly what you want, the Auzet bakers can also supply made-to-order breads; these include bouilla-baisse bread, saffron bread, onion bread, apricot bread, and, for those who like nibbling monograms, personal-ized bread rolls. You name it, they bake it.)

Gerard led me past the naked shelves and down a ramp that took us into the baking area, a large, airy room, bright white under the fluorescent lights. In one corner was a dough-kneading bowl the size of an infants' paddling pool, and 50-kilo (110-pound) sacks of flour, from the ultrafine to the coarser, almost gritty stone-ground; against the walls, stainless steel three-decker ovens six feet tall; between the ovens, steel work tables on which roughly formed *boules* of dough had been arranged in neat lines. There was no decoration, no stool to sit on, no concession to comfort, nothing that wasn't necessary for the making of bread. It was a functional room, saved from sterility by the earthy, reassuring smell of flour, and by the smiles and whistling of the bakers who were working the early shift, from four a.m. to noon.

That morning there were three of them, dressed in white T-shirts and shorts, their fingers and hands already pale with a dusting of flour. They started to work while I watched. I was at first surprised, then fascinated.

I was surprised because I had always thought that the standard loaves were formed mechanically, by some kind of molding process. I imagined a conveyor belt with dough going in at one end and *baguettes* coming out at the other—*baguettes* of identical size, identical weight, identical color, identical markings. I'm sure there are bread factories where this is exactly what happens, but it's not the way they do things at Auzet.

Every loaf is formed by hand, *façonnage à la main,* and it's a wonderful sight to behold. The preweighed lumps of dough (250 grams per *baguette*—a little more than half a pound) are taken, one by one, and slapped, rolled, squeezed, folded, and tweaked until they assume the familiar shape—if not yet the familiar color—of a loaf you would recognize on the shelf. It's like high-speed sculpture. The shaping of each loaf takes no more than thirty seconds, and after watching a dozen or so, you would swear that there are no differences between one loaf and the next. But of course, there are: the tiny variations, marks of humanity, that distinguish hand-made objects from those turned out by machine.

The variations are a little easier to spot at the next stage of the loaf's birth, when the decorative touches are added. With the classic *baguette,* for example, you will find a series of diagonal stripes along the top surface of the loaf. At Auzet, these are made by hand. They start as gashes, swift stabs with what I originally thought must be a special tool—the baker's friend—used only by the pros. When I asked to take a look at one, I saw that it was a sliver of tin clipped from a can, sharp and shiny from years of use.

In a matter of minutes, twenty lumps of dough had

become twenty *baguettes*. After each had been given its stripes, it was put on a length of flour-dusted canvas that had been corrugated to separate one loaf from the next. When the batch was completed, it was slid into the oven on a long wooden board.

By the time the first contingent of *baguettes* came out of the ovens, it was about four-thirty. The loaves were golden, some slightly darker at each end. Baking had caused the gashes to widen and fill in until they looked like indentations that might have been made in the crust by a finger applied horizontally across the loaf.

Gerard took a *baguette* from the batch and held it to his nose, much as a sommelier might check a cork. Then he turned the *baguette* over and tapped the flat underside two or three times, making a sound like a muffled drum-beat. "That's one way of testing the bread," he said. "You can hear when it's been baked correctly."

He passed me the loaf, and I gave it a novice's tap. Now that warm air had expanded the dough, the *baguette* felt light, almost hollow, rather than dense. I gave it a squeeze: firm, but yielding. I gave it a sniff. Mmmm. It made me wonder what time bakers had breakfast. I hoped it was soon.

This particular loaf, the standard, slim, everyday

baguette, is best eaten young. It stays fresh for four or five hours, no more. ("Too good to last," as Gerard would tell you.) And so it's not unusual for a baker to see many of his morning customers turn up again in the afternoon, when they come by to collect their dinner *baguettes.* Larger loaves stay fresh longer, as do the denser breads like *pain de campagne, pain au son,* and *pain complet.* But the *baguette* remains the most popular loaf, and indeed one of the enduring symbols of France.

Some years ago, this sacred object came under attack. Certain unscrupulous supermarkets, in an effort to seduce the trusting housewife and undercut local bakers, brought out the one-franc *baguette.* It was an inferior specimen, *bien sûr,* a miserable copy, but less than half the price of the real thing.

The supermarkets should have known better. Nobody trifles with the bakers of France, and war broke out at once. *Aux armes, les boulangers!* Independent bakers, united against a common foe, counterattacked. Delegations were sent to Paris. Ministers were petitioned. Protests were lodged in high places. The honor of French bread, the very fabric of French life, was at stake.

Finally, a group of bakers (among them Roger

Auzet, Gerard's father) came up with a method of identifying bread that had been made in the traditional way with traditional ingredients. It was a kind of trademark, a guarantee of superior quality. Banette was the chosen name, and you will see it today displayed on bags and signs in every *boulangerie* where proper bread is made.

BY FIVE A.M., the Auzet bakers were in overdrive, working with extraordinary speed and precision—

A small selection of the day's work

rolling and shaping the dough, slashing away with their miniature daggers, sliding the batches into the oven, thumping the oven doors shut. By the end of the day, more than a thousand loaves and *petits pains* would be formed, baked, and sold.

It was just after six when Gerard felt we deserved our breakfast. Leaving the bakers to their noble work, we went up the ramp and into the public part of the Auzet establishment, which over the years has become an informal mixture of shop, café, and art gallery. There are chairs and marble-topped tables along one wall where you can have coffee and a *croissant* still glowing from the warm breath of the oven. Posters by local artists, photographs, and mementos share wall space with shelves lined with bottles of champagne, pots of homemade jams and syrups, baskets of almond biscuits, flasks of truffle-scented olive oil.

And then there's the bread—a panorama of bread, stretching for perhaps twenty feet behind the counter, bread arranged according to type and size, varying in color from pale gold to a deep chocolate brown, a display as tanned and tightly packed as rows of sunbathers on a Riviera beach.

Once the shelves are filled, tables and chairs are set

Véronique Auzet. The smile lasts all day.

out on the pavement. It's taken for granted that the sun will shine all day, just as it has been doing for the past three months. Outdoor blinds and shutters are folded back from the display window, and the first soft gray light of dawn seeps into the shop. The door is fixed open. Chez Auzet is ready for business.

Six-fifteen, and the hollow feeling of being up so early begins to disappear, thanks to a *café crème* and a warm breakfast roll spread with almost-white butter and dipped into the coffee, a messy but delicious combination of tastes and textures.

The first customer of the day appears, trailing behind him a large paper sack. He is from the Hôtel du Parc at the end of the street and, this being August, the hotel is full. He leaves with a basket of *croissants* and a bulging sack of *baguettes*. Almost before he's out of the door, the gaps on the shelf are filled with more bread.

More customers arrive, the early-morning regulars, and they observe the daily ritual of handshakes and multiple kisses and enquiries after each other's health. The young women behind the counter wrap each purchase in a twist of paper with a dexterous turn of the wrist. Gerard circulates among his clients and rearranges a couple of loaves that have tilted sideways on the shelf. Symmetry restored to his satisfaction, he disappears down the ramp to commune with the ovens.

For him, it will be a long day. The early-morning batch is the first of many, and while a second shift of bakers will take over at noon, Gerard will stay until closing time, around six. He'll drive home to Ménerbes, have dinner with his family, get to bed around ten, and be up again at three the next morning. I ask him how he does it. "You get used to it," he says. But I think there's more to it than that. I think you have to have baker's genes.

Flour in the Blood

WHEN Marcel Pagnol wrote *"Je suis né dans le pétrin"*—I was born in the dough trough—he might have been describing any one of four generations of the Auzet family. For more than a hundred years, the Auzet men have been bakers.

Unfortunately, history in Provence is sometimes not passed on with as much detail or accuracy as one might wish. But we do have an idea of how it was to work as a baker during the second half of the nineteenth century, when Great-grandfather Auzet, born in 1845, was a young man.

His nickname was "l'Ortolan," although nobody knows why. The *ortolan* is a bird, a bunting, once much loved by gourmets until it became a protected species. It is tiny, no more than a mouthful of a bird, and it is hard to find any immediate resemblance to Great-grandfather Auzet. He is remembered as *un homme robuste*, broad-shouldered and muscular, who wore his baker's apron slung beneath his belly (an impressive belly, by all accounts, described in appropriate baking terms as the *brioche croissante*).

He was a traveling baker, making his way along the backcountry roads from farm to farm and village to village throughout the Luberon with his mule and his cart. By his side was a large jug filled with *eau de vie* to ward off the chill of the winter mistral, and a generous supply of precious and all-important *levain*. This is the starter, a mixture of natural yeasts and other micro-organisms. It takes time to make, sometimes as much as twenty days. But it is the heart and backbone of good bread, the element of fermentation that, when added to dough, causes it to rise and gives it lightness and flavor. It is one of the oldest examples in the world of gastro-nomic magic.

With his *levain* and his skill, Great-grandfather Auzet would stop at each farm on his route, and turn the farmer's flour into a batch of bread before moving on to his next call. In villages, he would use the communal oven. Wherever he went, he brought *un peu de bonheur*,

Great-grandfather Auzet

leaving behind him a trail of warm and aromatic kitchens. Not surprisingly, he was a popular visitor.

He had a son, Baptistin, who took up his father's *métier*, although by this time the traveling baker was being replaced by the stationary *boulangerie*. Baptistin set up shop in the shadow of the Cavaillon cathedral, making bread the way his father had made it.

Those were the days when farmers came into town each week with their fruit and vegetables, their chickens and rabbits, to sell them at the market in the Place du Clos. Transport was slow and four-legged, either mule

Roger Auzet, far left, 1941

or horse, and the journey into Cavaillon started well before dawn. Illumination on the pitch black roads was provided by an oil lamp, *le fanau*, hung on the side of the cart. Gerard Auzet's father remembers, as a boy, traveling with an elderly uncle from Lagnes to Cavaillon on one of those predawn expeditions. The lamp was lit, the cart set off—and the old man went to sleep. The horse was left in charge of the navigation. He was so accustomed to the route that he even knew his master's favorite café, where he would stop when he finally reached town.

Another generation took over in 1939, when Roger Auzet put on his apron and learned his craft. By 1947, he had his own *boulangerie* in Oppède, moving to the present site in Cavaillon in 1951. He is retired now, but he still visits the bakery, keeping an eye on things, glancing occasionally at a photograph on the wall that commemorates a high point in his long career.

Fifty years after starting to work as a baker, at a time when most men would be happy to leave the heat of the ovens and retire, Roger decided to give himself another challenge. He would compete for the grand prize of baking, to become the baker's baker, a *Meilleur Ouvrier de France*.

Auẓet fils et père—*Gerard and Roger*

No baker can even attempt this without a total mastery of technique. But to win the competition, he must also be a sculptor in dough, able to create *une pièce artistique*. To do so, he can choose any subject—a face, an animal, an arrangement of flowers, a bunch of grapes, a musical instrument, even a building. Roger's choice was, in fact, a building of sorts—the Eiffel Tower, which had just reached its hundredth anniversary.

It is hard to imagine the patience and the talent

required to make a scale model of something so detailed and complex in any material, let alone dough. It is difficult enough using wood or metal, which are at least rigid; it must be infinitely more difficult using soft, malleable dough that needs not only to be perfectly formed but also perfectly baked. One slip of the fingers, a miscalculation of the oven temperature, and all that remains is a deformed lump.

Roger's technical description of the building of the tower is more like an engineer's blueprint than an artistic brief:

> Make a cardboard template to the scaled-down dimensions of the tower—four sides measuring 9 inches by 23 3/4 inches. Cover with cooking paper, glued and lined inside with pressed paper to avoid any deformation during cooking. Make the four sides and cook them, joining them together with a thin strip of dough. Place each side in the freezer as soon as it is finished.
>
> Bake in a rotating oven with the initial temperature at 180°C [350°F]. Switch off, and leave for forty-five minutes. The edges of the different levels should be baked separately, as should

La Tour Auzet

the inside of the tower, and stuck on with food paste.

Add decorations to represent the cobbles around the base, and, to celebrate the tower's centenary, a crown of flowers. Finally, add some sheaves of wheat to symbolize the baker's profession. *Et voilà.*

The result was a masterpiece, and Roger won his prize. Alas for the tower, it was knocked over while on display in the shop. But the photograph, the medal, and the distinction remain, a tribute to a man's passion for his work.

If you have an uncomfortable feeling that someone has put a spell on you, the remedy is available at your nearest *boulangerie.* Wrap a piece of bread in a clean white napkin, give it to the first person you meet in the morning.
The spell will be lifted.

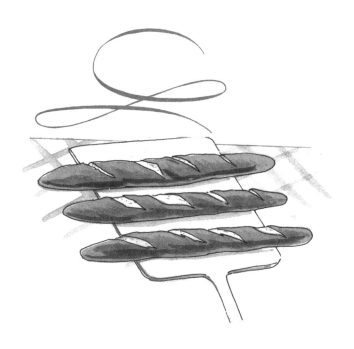

The Breads, the Recipes,
the Tricks of the Trade

PEOPLE who are truly expert at what they do tend to suffer from a disarming form of modesty. They make their hard-earned skill or God-given knack sound almost effortless. Nothing to it, really, they say. I could teach you to do it in no time.

It's a seductive theory, and I have been optimistic enough to believe it on several occasions: horseback riding, computer literacy, rose pruning, omelette making—these are just a few of the accomplishments that I was told I could master by following a handful of simple directions. Each time I followed as best I could. Each time my efforts were crowned by failure.

Now here I am with another expert, Gerard Auzet, and he tells me that anyone can make good bread.

"Even me?" I ask him.

He looks at me for a moment, and I can sense a certain amount of quite justifiable doubt. And yet, finally, he nods. "Even you," he says.

He goes on to explain that successful baking is largely a question of using only the best ingredients—*nobles, sains, et frais* are his exact words (noble, healthy, and fresh)—of arming yourself with some basic equipment, and of having the ability to count up to 56. This is 56° centigrade, the combined temperature of the air in the kitchen, the flour, and the water. For example: If the temperature in the kitchen is 20°C and the flour is 22°C, then the water needs to be 14°C. A degree or so of difference among these three doesn't matter as long as the total adds up to 56. And if your ingredients are as they should be, the rest, according to Gerard, is simple. Alas, that's not quite the case once you cross the Atlantic. In America we have found that conversions to the rule of 56 just don't work, perhaps because of the ingredients or higher temperatures in the kitchen. That's why we specify Fahrenheit temperatures (and American measures) in all the recipes.

You will need a set of kitchen scales, an oven with a good thick *plaque*, or hot plate, white Type 55 or Type

65 flour,* table salt, some baker's yeast, and pure water. You are now ready to attack the recipes. These, as you will see, start with the plain classic breads, but also include some slightly more complicated and ambitious variations using herbs and spices, fruit and nuts. Don't let these intimidate you. Once you have the basic baking technique under control, all things are possible.

"Le pain est l'une des plus belles créations de l'homme."

In the bad old days of the fourteenth century, when the popes ruled from their palace in Avignon, the penalty for making substandard bread was severe. The guilty baker would have most of his clothes removed before being tied up in front of his shop, and then the good people of Avignon were encouraged to hit him with a stick as they passed by. The quality of his bread tended to improve dramatically.

*In this book, for American use, we used King Arthur Bread Flour and King Arthur All-Purpose Flour, half and half.

boule

fougasse

braid

batard

tree

Bread According to
Gerard Auzet

GOOD BREAD is one of the oldest pleasures on earth, so if you stick carefully to the recipes that follow you will be in the happy position of making pleasure—pleasure for yourself, for your family, and for your friends.

The products used in these recipes are all natural ingredients that have been linked for centuries to mankind's food and culture. Many of them were first used in baking generations ago, when peasants who made their own bread took baking a step beyond flour and water by adding other ingredients, among them olives, cheese, thyme, walnuts, bacon, and milk. These were grown or raised on their farms and found their way into the bread, thus adding variety and interest to what was usually a very simple daily diet.

In Gerard's recipes, he has chosen ingredients that add to the taste without overpowering the basic flavor of the bread. To approximate the white flour he uses, we had to use two flours: King Arthur Bread Flour and King Arthur All-Purpose Flour, mixed half and half. The substitution works. Not even a Frenchman could taste the difference.

As for the look of the loaf, here are two tips:

- When cutting your loaf with a razor to decorate it, never cut deeply; keep the blade flat, so that you just cut the surface of the loaf.

- By all means use a water spray on your bread when it is in the oven, to encourage a handsome crust. But make sure you keep the oven door closed for several minutes afterward so that the steam can't escape.

And here is a simple test to check that your bread is ready:

- Tap the bottom of the loaf with your knuckles. If the bread is fully baked, you should hear a hollow sound.

You are now ready for what Gerard, when he's feeling lyrical, refers to as "the magic of creation." Enjoy it.

When normal methods of village diplomacy in Provence came to nothing, bread was the last resort. Once a year, on Christmas morning, villagers would take bread they had baked to the fountain, leave it on the edge of the *bassin,* and take away a loaf made by a neighbor. This was said to renew good relations between inhabitants who had fallen out with one another during the year.

Essential Items for the Advanced Baker

S REWARDING as it is to make your own *baguettes* and *boules*, there will probably come a time when you will want to expand your repertoire, venture beyond the everyday loaf, and try your hand at some of the more popular highly seasoned breads—the *pain aux olives*, the *pain aux oignons*, the *pain à l'ail*. For these, you will need the ingredients listed below.

It goes without saying that these should be the best you can find. Unlike wine, they do not improve with age, and nothing is as disappointing as bread made with oil that has long since lost its virginal youth, elderly and wizened olives, or last year's garlic. So be firm, and insist that everything you use is fresh.

Olives and Olive Oil

For many people, the olive is merely an accessory to the aperitif, to be enjoyed with a glass of something chilled and delicious. But a baker sees olives as jewels set in bread—green and juicy, or dark, fat, and rich, with just the right hint of bitterness, they look wonderfully picturesque and appetizing dotted into a plump loaf. You will find that Gerard Auzet and other distinguished bakers are generous both with the quantity of olives used and the size of the pieces. Mean little slivers are forbidden. Chunks or thick slices are recommended. And if you want to stick to the Auzet recipe, the olives should be from Provence.

As for the oil, it must be young, cold-pressed, and extra-virgin (while an impossible condition in humans, the latter phrase is used to identify oil with an acidity of less than one percent).

Onions

This is very much a question of personal taste, or *chacun à son oignon*. Some people like the chopped onions in their bread to be crunchy and almost raw, with a discernible bite. Others prefer their onions simmered in oil and butter, sweet, melting, and subtle. A few sessions of enjoyable experimentation—preferably in the company of your greediest friends—will tell you which suits you best.

Garlic

The Egyptian laborers building the Pyramids once went on strike because their garlic ration was late in being delivered. Athenian wrestlers and Roman gladiators ate raw garlic as an aid to strength and courage. And even the most modern medical techniques have failed to discover a more effective vampire deterrent than a clove of garlic. In the hands of a skilled baker, this most potent member of the onion family can add a delicious and distinctive tang to bread. In unskilled hands, it can taste sour, overpowering, and dreadful—to be used with caution. Note: If there is a *germe,* or tiny green sprout, in the middle of the clove, it should be removed.

Saffron

Included here for real enthusiasts, saffron comes from the stigmas of the crocus flower. These have to be picked by hand, and it takes seventy thousand flowers to make approximately five hundred grams or a little more than half a pound, so it is, not surprisingly, the most expensive of spices. Fortunately, a little goes a very long way. Saffron-flavored bread is ideal with bouillabaisse (which is why Gerard calls it *pain bouillabaisse*), but if you like the taste of saffron it's also good with the most humble of fish soups, or indeed with any pilaf, paella, or risotto that requires saffron in its recipe.

ONCE YOU HAVE mastered these variations on the basic loaf, your baking ambitions may well extend to even more exotic flavors: anchovies, walnuts, Roquefort, bacon, thyme, almonds—bread is a wonderful background for all of these different tastes and textures. As with olives, onions, and garlic, use the very best ingredients you can find. Recipes are provided here, but you may want to take the time to experiment with quantities until you find a balance that exactly matches your own taste. And then, not forgetting to kiss the tips of your fingers, you can say as you offer it to your friends, "This is *my* bread."

In those long-ago days before the coming of the bagel, the Jews of Provence had their own particular breads. One took the form of a round, cakelike loaf, made by throwing the dough into oil before smothering it in jam and eating it. Another, baked in the form of a ladder, was traditionally covered with a spread made of honey and cherries.

Traditional Bread Dough

Baguettes, Boules, et Bâtards

Baguettes

Makes about 2 pounds of dough, enough to
make 4 15-inch *baguettes*

3 1/2 cups (16 ounces) unbleached all-purpose flour
1 1/2 teaspoons (1/4 ounce) salt
4 1/2 teaspoons (1/2 ounce) instant yeast
1 1/4 cups (10 ounces) water (90–100°F)

1. Sift the flour and salt together into the bowl
of a standing mixer fitted with the dough hook.
Sprinkle the yeast over the mixture and mix
on medium to low speed, gradually adding the

water, until the dough comes away from the bowl, in 5–10 minutes.

2. Remove the dough from the mixing bowl, and set it on the counter to rest for 10 minutes. Return it to the mixing bowl and set on the mixer so that the dough hook plunges into the middle of the dough. Mix on medium speed until the dough is soft and pliable, about 15–20 minutes, or until the dough passes the "windowpane" test. (See page 45.)

3. Remove the dough from the mixing bowl onto the counter and gather it up in your hands in a rough ball. The dough should feel soft.

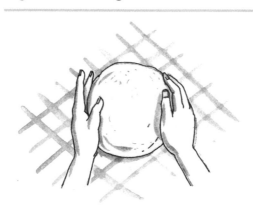

Bring the full length of your thumbs into the center of the ball so that they meet, and stretch the dough from the center out, as if opening a book, into an oblong shape.

Turn the dough a quarter turn and stretch it again the same way, creating a smooth ball. Transfer the dough to a large mixing bowl, cover with plastic wrap or a damp kitchen towel, and set aside in a draft-free place at room temperature until the dough doubles in size, about 45 minutes.

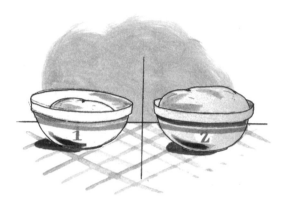

4. Gently remove the dough from the bowl and place it on a clean surface. Cut the dough into 4 pieces and shape into 4 smooth *bâtards* (you will shape them into *baguettes* later) by stretching out the dough from the center only once, to maintain an oblong shape. Find a surface in your kitchen free from drafts and lay a kitchen towel dusted with flour on it. Place the *bâtards* on the kitchen towel and cover with plastic wrap or with another kitchen towel, this one a little bit damp, to prevent a crust from form-

ing on the surface. Leave the loaves to proof at room temperature until they double in size, 20–25 minutes.

5. Shape the loaves by lifting them off the towel and stretching them out from the ends. Use the side of your hand to create a crease down the middle of the dough. Fold the dough onto itself at the crease, pressing it firmly against the work surface to seal it. Using the palms of your hands and working from the center of the dough out, gently roll it back and forth until it stretches to 15 inches long.

6. Place the loaves, seam-side down, on the kitchen towel dusted with flour and cover with plastic wrap or a damp kitchen towel. Let the loaves rise at room temperature for the final time, until they have doubled in size, about 35–45 minutes.

7. Meanwhile, preheat the oven to 475°F. Carefully place the loaves on a baking sheet. Brush them with water using a pastry brush. With a sharp razor blade and swift motions, make 4 or 5 diagonal slashes along the length of each *baguette*. To do this successfully, do not drag the

entire edge of the blade through the dough—use just the tip.

8. Just before you are ready to slide the baking sheet into the oven, spray the inside of the oven with water using a spray bottle or plant mister and close the door immediately. This will create steam, which promotes a good crust. Put the bread in the oven and spray the walls of the oven two more times within the first minute of baking. Bake for 15–20 minutes or until the bread makes a hollow sound when you knock on the bottom of it with your knuckles. Transfer the bread to a rack and allow it to cool before slicing (or tearing a piece off).

How to Perform the Windowpane Test

When you knead bread dough, either by hand or in a mixer, you are developing the glutens, which are the proteins in wheat that give bread its structure and flavor. When the glutens are properly developed, the resulting bread will have that yeasty flavor and the irregular pockets that are the marks of a good loaf. To determine whether the glutens have been fully developed, pull off from the dough a piece about the size of a golf ball. Stretch, pull, and turn it, thinning the dough until it forms a translucent membrane (so you can see light passing through it, but not so that you create a hole), or windowpane. If the dough falls apart before it can be stretched into a windowpane, continue kneading several minutes more and repeat the test.

An old phrase says: "If you meet a baker
in the street, *monsieur,* raise your hat.
He deserves respect."

Boules et Bâtards

This recipe makes two traditional French *boules,* or balls, each about 8 inches in diameter, or *bâtards,* the popular torpedo-shaped loaves, each anywhere from 6 to 10 inches long. Gerard uses a basic ingredient combination—1 pound of flour, 1 1/2 teaspoons of salt, 1 tablespoon plus 1 teaspoon of instant yeast, and 10 ounces of liquid— to make the basic breads his family has been baking for generations. By varying the combination of liquids (water, wine, and olive oil, for example) and adding dried fruits, nuts, olives, herbs, onions, garlic, or sweet pumpkin, you can make delicious variations, both savory and sweet. The dough may also be shaped into ladders *(fougasse)* and braids *(épi)*. All of the breads here are based on this basic recipe, but I've grouped them according to the liquid additions that distinguish them: water, water and wine, water and olive oil, and, in the case of the sweet breads, butter, and given a basic recipe for each. All of

Gerard's breads are best eaten the day they are made.

Makes about 2 pounds of dough, enough to
make 2 *boules*, 8 inches in diameter, or 2 10- to
12-inches-long *bâtards*

1 3/4 cups (8 ounces) unbleached all-purpose flour
1 3/4 cups (8 ounces) unbleached bread flour
1 1/2 teaspoons (1/4 ounce) salt
4 1/2 teaspoons (1/2 ounce) instant yeast
1 1/4 cups (10 ounces) water (90–100°F)

1. Sift the flour and salt together into the bowl
of a standing mixer fitted with the dough hook.
Sprinkle the yeast over the mixture and mix on
medium to low speed, gradually adding the
water, until the dough comes away from the
bowl, in 5–10 minutes.

2. Remove the dough from the mixing bowl,
and set it on the counter to rest for 10 minutes.
Return it to the mixing bowl and set on the mixer
so that the dough hook plunges into the middle of

the dough. Mix on medium speed until the dough is soft and pliable, about 15–20 minutes, or until the dough passes the "windowpane" test. (See page 45.)

3. Remove the dough from the mixing bowl onto the counter and gather it up in your hands in a rough ball. The dough should feel soft. Bring the full length of your thumbs into the center of the ball so that they meet, and stretch the dough from the center out, as if opening a book, into an oblong shape. Turn the dough a quarter turn and stretch it again the same way, creating a smooth ball. Transfer the dough to a large mixing bowl, cover with plastic wrap or a damp kitchen towel, and set aside in a draft-free place at room temper-

A Simple Test for the First Rise

If you can't tell if the dough has doubled in size, poke your thumb into it. If the indentation remains, the dough is ready. If it springs back, the dough hasn't risen sufficiently.

ature until the dough doubles in size, about 45 minutes.

4. Gently remove the dough from the bowl and place it on a clean surface. Cut the dough into 2 pieces (about 1 pound each) and shape them into 2 smooth balls again, as you did before the first rise. Find a surface in your kitchen free from drafts and lay a kitchen towel dusted with flour on it. Place the balls on the towel and cover them with plastic wrap or a damp towel to prevent a crust from forming on the surface. Leave the loaves to proof at room temperature until they double in size, in about 20–25 minutes.

5. Shape the loaves by first patting down the balls to allow the carbonic gasses that have developed to disperse. To make *boules,* gather up the dough in a rough ball and shape as in Step 3. To make *bâtards,* pat down the dough and shape it into a rough 4-by-10-inch rectangle. (See illustration on page 50.) With a long side facing you, fold the bottom third of the dough to the center and press to seal it. Fold the top over it and seal along the edge.

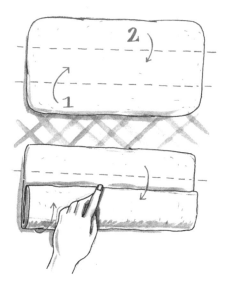

6. Place the loaves, seam side down, on the kitchen towel dusted with flour and cover with plastic wrap or a damp towel. Let the loaves rise at room temperature for the final time, until they have doubled in size, about 35–45 minutes.

7. Meanwhile, preheat the oven to 450°F. Carefully place the loaves on a baking sheet. Brush them with water using a pastry brush. With a sharp razor blade, make a lozenge-shaped cut on the surface of each loaf by scoring it from

end to end in 2 swift motions. To do this successfully, use just the tip of the blade.

8. Just before you are ready to slide the baking
sheet into the oven, spray the inside of the oven
with water using a spray bottle or plant mister
and close the door immediately. This will create
steam, which promotes a good crust. Put the
bread in the oven and bake for 20–25 minutes or
until the bread makes a hollow sound when you
knock on the bottom of it with your knuckles.
Transfer the bread to a rack and allow it to cool
before slicing.

Thyme Bread

Pain au Thym

These loaves, dotted throughout with fresh thyme leaves, fill the kitchen with the unmistakable fragrance of Provence, where this bread is a standard selection at Auzet's bakery. Enjoy it with goat cheese or for sopping up the juices of a main course meat dish prepared in a sauce.

Additional step: Add ¾ cup of fresh thyme leaves to the dough once it has come away from the sides of the mixing bowl in Step 1. Continue to mix the dough until the thyme leaves are incorporated.

How to Make Leaf-Shaped Loaves

These pretty loaves are made by making deep cuts with a sharp pair of scissors into dough that has been shaped into *bâtards*. Cut the loaves just before they go into the oven.

Pumpkin Bread

Pain au Potiron

Tiny cubes of sweet pumpkin seasoned with black pepper make these savory peasant loaves excellent for dunking into soup. In fact, in the countryside, dried slices of pumpkin bread are preferred for soaking up every last bit of soup broth.

Additional step: Season 1 1/4 cups (1/2 pound) of diced sweet pumpkin or butternut squash with freshly ground black pepper. Add the pumpkin to the dough after it passes the windowpane test in Step 3. Put the pumpkin into the mixing bowl and mix just until incorporated.

Just after brushing the loaf with water, turn it so one of the pointed or short sides is facing you. Cut into the center of the loaf on the diagonal—without cutting through the center—along the length of the loaf (about three cuts on either side should do it). You will essentially be making a series of upside-down Vs. Bake the bread as directed.

The invention of the *croissant*, so they say, dates from August 26, 1683. It happened in Vienna, which was then under siege by the Turkish army. That night, a team of bakers working the early shift heard suspicious noises that seemed to be coming from the ground beneath their feet. They raised the alarm, and a search party captured a group of Turkish soldiers in the act of placing mines under the city's fortifications and powder magazine. It was the final setback for the Turks. The siege was lifted and the army went home. To celebrate the end of the siege, the bakers of Vienna decided to make bread in the form of the crescent that appears on the Turkish flag. This was the original *croissant*, which now exists only in Austria. Its modern descendant, made with flaky pastry, was introduced in 1920, and has been a French specialty ever since.

Apricot and Hazelnut Bread

Pain aux Abricots et Noisettes

A pat of butter or a spoonful of jam, honey, or hazelnut spread is all you need to turn a thick slice of this slightly sweet bread into breakfast or an afternoon snack with a cup of tea. Or, spoil your friends (and yourself) by lightly frying or grilling some slices and serving them with foie gras.

Additional step: Add 1 cup coarsely chopped hazelnuts and ¾ cup dried apricots diced into ¼-inch pieces to the dough after it passes the windowpane test in Step 3. Scatter the nuts and apricots evenly over the dough and mix just until incorporated.

Roquefort Bread

Pain au Roquefort

This is one of Gerard's more sophisticated—and addictive—loaves, the kind you find yourself slicing from (or just pulling off a piece) all day long. It is a delicious accompaniment to green salads and grilled meats. Let the Roquefort soften completely before you add it to the dough. Note: Because the cheese imparts moisture to the dough, add only 5/8 cup of water (90–100°F) to the dry ingredients in Step 1.

Additional step: Add 5 1/4 ounces of softened Roquefort to the dough after it comes away from the sides of the bowl in Step 1. Continue to mix the dough until the cheese is incorporated.

Garlic Bread

Pain à l'Ail

Tiny cubes of sautéed garlic are mixed right into the dough of these universally appealing loaves. Almost any cheese tastes better accompanied by a few warm slices of this garlic bread. Be sure to use the very freshest garlic available, and dice it—don't crush it. Note: Add only 1 cup of water (90–100°F) to the dry ingredients in Step 1 to make this slightly stiffer dough.

Additional step: Dice 6 cloves of garlic into 1/8-inch pieces. Toss the tiny cubes in a tablespoon of flour until they are well coated. Scatter them evenly in the mixing bowl after the dough has pulled away from the sides in Step 1. Continue to mix until the garlic is incorporated.

Breads Made with Wine

Walnut and Red Wine Bread

Pain aux Noix et Vin Rouge

Adding chopped walnuts generously to this special bread ensures that you will get some in every rose-toned slice. It is an ideal companion to cheeses of all kinds and is the perfect accompaniment to a simple green salad dressed with olive oil.

Makes 2 loaves

1 3/4 cups (8 ounces) unbleached all-purpose flour
1 3/4 cups (8 ounces) unbleached bread flour
1 1/2 teaspoons (1/4 ounce) salt
5/8 cup (5 ounces) water (90–100°F)

⅝ cup (5 ounces) red wine
4 ½ teaspoons (½ ounce) instant yeast
2 cups (12 ounces) coarsely chopped walnuts

1. Sift the flour and salt together into the bowl of a standing mixer fitted with the dough hook. Sprinkle the yeast over the mixture and mix on medium to low speed, gradually adding the water and wine, until the dough comes away from the bowl, between 5 and 10 minutes. Scatter the walnuts evenly over the dough and continue mixing until they are incorporated.

2. Remove the dough from the mixing bowl and set it on the counter to rest for 10 minutes. Return it to the mixing bowl and place on mixer so the dough hook plunges into the middle of the dough. Mix on medium speed until the dough is soft and pliable, about 15–20 minutes or until the dough passes the "windowpane" test. (See page 45.)

3. Remove the dough from the mixing bowl onto a counter and gather it up in your hands in a rough ball. Bring the full length of your thumbs into the center of the ball so that they meet, and

stretch the dough from the center out, as if opening a book, into an oblong shape. Turn the dough a quarter turn and stretch the dough again the same way, creating a smooth ball. Transfer the dough to a large mixing bowl, cover with plastic wrap or a damp kitchen towel, and set aside in a draft-free place at room temperature until the dough doubles in size, in about 45 minutes.

4. Gently remove the dough from the bowl and place it on a clean surface. Cut the dough into 2 pieces (about 1 pound each) and shape it into 2 smooth balls again, as you did before the first rise. Find a surface in your kitchen free from drafts and lay a kitchen towel dusted with flour on it. Place the balls on the towel and cover with plastic wrap or a damp towel to prevent a crust from forming on the surface. Leave the loaves to proof at room temperature until they double in size, in about 20–25 minutes.

5. Shape the loaves by first patting down the balls to allow the carbonic gasses that have developed to disperse. To make *boules*, gather up the dough in a rough ball and shape it as in Step 3. To make *bâtards*, pat down the dough and shape it

into a rough 4-by-10-inch rectangle. With a long side facing you, fold the bottom third of the dough to the center and press to seal it. Fold the top over it and seal along the edge.

6. Place the loaves, seam side down, on the kitchen towel dusted with flour and cover with plastic wrap or a damp towel. Let the loaves rise at room temperature for the final time until they have doubled in size, about 35–45 minutes.

7. Meanwhile, preheat the oven to 450°F. Carefully place the loaves on a baking sheet. Brush them with water using a pastry brush. With a sharp razor blade, make a lozenge-shaped cut on the surface of each loaf by scoring it from end to end in 2 swift motions. To do this successfully, use just the tip of the blade.

8. Just before you are ready to slide the baking sheet into the oven, spray the inside of the oven with water using a spray bottle or plant mister and close the door immediately. This will create steam, which promotes a good crust. Put the bread in the oven and bake for 20–25 minutes or until it makes a hollow sound when you knock on

the bottom of it with your knuckles. Transfer the bread to a rack and allow it to cool before slicing.

Variations:

For all of the breads made with wine, the ratio of liquid to dry ingredients remains the same and the amount will always total 1 ¼ cups. The quantity of each liquid will vary from recipe to recipe.

Onion and White Wine Bread
Pain aux Oignons et Vin Blanc

Lightly sautéed onions and white wine delicately flavor this bread, a good one for toasting and dunking into a bowl of hot soup. Note: Some of the wine in this recipe is used to deglaze the pan in which the onions are sautéed.

Ingredient preparation: Before you begin mixing the dough, melt 2 tablespoons of butter over medium-low heat. Add 1 1/2 cups of diced onions (about 2 small ones) and sauté, stirring occasionally, until they are soft and slightly golden. Deglaze the pan with 1/4 cup of white wine. Drain the onions, reserving the liquid. Set both aside to cool.

Liquid substitution: Pour the cooking liquid into a measuring cup and add enough white wine to make 5/8 cup. Add it and 5/8 cup of water to the dry ingredients.

Additional step: Add the sautéed onions after the dough passes the windowpane test in Step 2. Continue mixing until they are incorporated.

Winemaker's Bread

Pain au Vigneron

Dense with savory nuts and sweet raisins, this bread is popular among Gerard's customers during the autumn months. It makes wonderful breakfast toast, slathered with butter, jam, or honey.

Liquid substitution: Add ¾ cup of red wine plus ½ cup of water to the dry mixture.

Additional step: Omit the walnuts and instead add ⅓ cup each of raisins, chopped almonds, and chopped hazelnuts plus 2 tablespoons each of pine nuts and pistachio nuts to the dough just after it comes away from the bowl in Step 1.

Bacon Bread

Pain au Bacon

Crispy bits of sautéed bacon flavor this country loaf, which is substantial enough to stand up to such hearty dishes as choucroute and cassoulet.

Ingredient preparation: Cut 7 ounces of bacon into ½-inch-by-¼-inch strips. Fry the bacon in a skillet over high heat until crisp. Drain the fat. Add ¾ cup of white wine to the pan and bring to a boil. Drain, reserving the liquid, and set aside the bacon and liquid to cool.

Liquid substitution: Pour the reserved cooking liquid into a measuring cup and add enough white wine to make ¾ cup. Add it and ½ cup of water to the dry ingredients.

Additional step: Add the drained bacon after the dough pulls away from the sides in Step 1. Continue mixing until the bacon is incorporated.

Always burn any bread crumbs that have fallen from the table. If you don't, there is a strong possibility that you will have to return after your death to spend eternity gathering up bread crumbs with your eyelids, or with a bottomless basket.

Breads Made with Olive Oil

Green and Black Olive Bread

Pain aux Olives

This is the kind of bread that you can't help but tear off a piece to eat for a snack. It is also a nice bread to cut up into small slices and serve on an hors d'oeuvre tray with cheeses, dips, and spreads. When a hearty meat dish is on the dinner menu, this is the bread to serve.

Makes 2 loaves

1 3/4 cups (8 ounces) unbleached all-purpose flour
1 3/4 cups (8 ounces) unbleached bread flour
1 1/2 teaspoons (1/4 ounce) salt
4 1/2 teaspoons (1/2 ounce) instant yeast

¾ cup (6 ounces) water (90–100°F)

½ cup (4 ounces) olive oil

¾ cup (4 ounces) pitted black olives

¾ cup (4 ounces) pitted green olives

2 tablespoons herbes de Provence

1. Sift the flour and salt together into the bowl of a standing mixer fitted with the dough hook. Sprinkle the yeast over the contents and mix on medium to low speed, gradually adding the water and the olive oil, until the dough comes away from the bowl, about 5–10 minutes. Scatter the olives and the herbs over the dough and continue mixing until they are incorporated.

2. Remove the dough from the mixing bowl, and set it on the counter to rest for 10 minutes. Return it to the mixing bowl and place on the mixer so the dough hook plunges into the middle of the dough. Mix on medium speed until the dough is soft and pliable, about 15–20 minutes or until the dough passes the windowpane test. (See page 45.)

3. Remove the dough from the mixing bowl to the counter and gather it up in your hands in a

rough ball. Bring the full length of your thumbs into the center of the ball so that they meet, and stretch the dough from the center out, as if opening a book, into an oblong shape. Turn the dough a quarter turn and stretch the dough again the same way, creating a smooth ball. Transfer the dough to a large mixing bowl, cover it with plastic wrap or a damp kitchen towel, and set it aside in a draft-free place at room temperature until the dough doubles in size, in about 45 minutes.

4. Gently remove the dough from the bowl and place it on a clean surface. Cut the dough into 2 pieces (about 1 pound each) and shape them into 2 smooth balls again, as you did before the first rise. Find a surface in your kitchen free from drafts and lay a kitchen towel dusted with flour on it. Place the balls on the towel and cover with plastic wrap or a damp towel to prevent a crust from forming on the surface. Leave the loaves to proof at room temperature until they double in size, in 20–25 minutes.

5. Shape the loaves by first patting down the balls to allow the carbonic gasses that have developed to disperse. To make *boules,* gather up the

dough in a rough ball and shape it as in Step 3. To make *bâtards*, pat down the dough and shape it into a rough 4-by-10-inch rectangle. With a long side facing you, fold the bottom third of the dough to the center and press to seal it. Fold the top over it and seal along the edge.

6. Place the loaves, seam side down, on the towel dusted with flour and cover with plastic wrap or a damp towel. Let the loaves rise at room temperature for the final time until they have doubled in size, in about 35–45 minutes.

7. Meanwhile, preheat the oven to 450°F. Carefully place the loaves on a baking sheet. Brush them with water using a pastry brush. Using a sharp razor blade, make a lozenge-shaped cut on the surface of each loaf by scoring it from end to end in 2 swift motions. To do this successfully, use just the tip of the blade.

8. Just before you are ready to slide the baking sheet into the oven, spray the inside of the oven with water using a spray bottle or plant mister and close the door immediately. This will create steam, which promotes a good crust. Put the bread in the oven and bake for 20–25 minutes or

until the bread makes a hollow sound when you knock on the bottom of it with your knuckles. Transfer the bread to a rack and allow it to cool before slicing.

Variation

Fisherman's Bread

Pain Bouillabaisse

Named for the soup that features the same flavors that infuse this bread—saffron, fennel, garlic, and *herbes de Provence*—this bread is delightful sliced, quartered, and grilled or fried, then topped with a filet of marinated fish or floating in fish soup. It is equally delicious spread with garlic mayonnaise *(Provençal aioli)*.

Additional step: Sift a pinch of saffron with the flour and salt.

Liquid substitutions: Add 3/4 cup water and 1/2 cup olive oil to the dry ingredients.

Additional steps: Add 2 teaspoons of fennel and 1 teaspoon of *herbes de Provence* to the mixture right after the liquid ingredients have been added. Add 1 tablespoon of diced garlic, dusted with flour, to the dough after it has passed the windowpane test in Step 2. Continue to mix until the garlic is incorporated.

To encourage children with
finicky appetites, parents would tell
them that if they ate all their bread,
even if it had begun to turn moldy,
they would be sure to find money
scattered in the bushes.

Sweet Yeast Breads

Milk Bread

Pain au Lait

Essentially breakfast bread—it's excellent toasted and spread with butter, jam, or honey—this loaf is rather compact, making it good for sandwiches, too. Gerard likes to eat a slice of this bread with ham and cheese, in particular, but doesn't shy away from slathering it with butter and melted chocolate. Milk Bread may be torpedo-shaped, or, for special occasions, twisted into braids.

Makes 2 loaves

1 ¾ cups (8 ounces) unbleached all-purpose flour
1 ¾ cups (8 ounces) unbleached bread flour

1 1/2 teaspoons (1/4 ounce) salt
4 1/2 teaspoons (1/2 ounce) instant yeast
1 tablespoon (1/2 ounce) softened butter
3 tablespoons (1 ounce) powdered milk
4 1/2 teaspoons sugar
1 cup (8 ounces) water (90–100°F)
Beaten egg, for glaze (optional)
Sesame seeds, for topping (optional)
Sugar, for topping (optional)

1. Sift the flour and salt together into the bowl of a standing mixer fitted with the dough hook. Sprinkle the yeast over the contents, drop the butter into the middle of the flour, and mix on medium to low speed, gradually putting in the powdered milk and sugar. Slowly add in the water and mix until the dough comes away from the bowl, in about 5–10 minutes.

2. Remove the dough from the bowl and set it on the counter to rest for 10 minutes. Return the dough to the bowl and place on mixer so the dough hook plunges into the middle of the dough. Mix on medium speed until the dough is

soft and pliable, about 15–20 minutes or until the dough passes the windowpane test. (See page 45.)

3. Remove the dough from the mixing bowl to the counter and gather it up in your hands in a rough ball. Bring the full length of your thumbs into the center of the ball so that they meet, and stretch the dough from the center out, as if opening a book, into an oblong shape. Turn the dough a quarter turn and stretch the dough again the same way, creating a smooth ball. Transfer the dough to a large mixing bowl, cover it with plastic wrap or a damp kitchen towel, and set it aside in a draft-free place at room temperature until the dough doubles in size, in about 45 minutes.

4. Gently remove the dough from the bowl and place it on a clean surface. Cut the dough into 2 pieces (about 1 pound each) and shape into 2 smooth balls again, as you did before the first rise. If you want to make braided loaves, cut the dough into 6 equal pieces and shape them into balls. Find a surface in your kitchen free from drafts and lay a kitchen towel dusted with flour on it. Place the balls on the kitchen towel and

cover with plastic wrap or a damp towel to prevent a crust from forming on the surface. Leave the loaves to proof at room temperature until they double in size, in 20–25 minutes.

5. Shape the loaves by first patting down the balls to allow the carbonic gasses that have developed to disperse. To make *bâtards,* pat down the dough and shape it into a rough 4-by-10-inch rectangle. With a long side facing you, fold the bottom third of the dough to the center and press to seal it. Fold the top over it and seal along the edge. To make a braided loaf, pull each of the six balls out lengthwise until they are about 8 inches long. If the dough resists, set it aside to rest for a few minutes. Working with 3 pieces at a time, connect them at 1 end by pinching them together. Beginning with the strand on the right, bring it up and over the middle strand, so that it becomes the middle strand. Next, bring the strand on the left up and over the middle strand. Continue bringing the right and left strands over the middle strand until you reach the end of the strands. Connect them at the end by pinching them together, as you did to begin the braid.

6. Place the loaves (seam side down if they are *bâtards*) on the kitchen towel dusted with flour and cover with plastic wrap or a damp towel. Let the loaves rise at room temperature for the final time, until they have doubled in size, about 35–45 minutes.

7. Meanwhile, preheat the oven to 425°F. Carefully place the loaves on a baking sheet. Brush them with water or the egg glaze using a pastry brush. Sprinkle the sesame seeds or sugar evenly on top, if using. Using a sharp razor blade, make a lozenge-shaped cut on the surface of each loaf by scoring it from end to end in 2 swift motions. To do this successfully, use just the tip of the blade.

8. Just before you are ready to slide the baking sheet into the oven, spray the inside of the oven with water using a spray bottle or plant mister and close the door immediately. This will create steam, which promotes a good crust. Put the bread in the oven and bake for 20 minutes for a soft bread, 25 minutes for a crustier bread. Transfer the bread to a rack and allow it to cool before slicing.

Ladder Bread

Fougasse

Though it looks like it requires special skills to make, *fougasse* is essentially a *bâtard* that is flattened, scored in a decorative pattern, and folded in half to enclose any number of sweet or savory fillings.

Makes 2 loaves

1 ¾ cups (8 ounces) unbleached all-purpose flour
1 ¾ cups (8 ounces) unbleached bread flour
1 ½ teaspoons (¼ ounce) salt
4 ½ teaspoons (½ ounce) instant yeast
1 tablespoon (½ ounce) softened butter
3 tablespoons (1 ounce) powdered milk
4 ½ teaspoons sugar
1 cup (8 ounces) water (90°–100°F)
Beaten egg for glaze (optional)
Sesame seeds, for topping (optional)
Sugar, for topping (optional)

1. Sift the flour and salt together into the bowl of a standing mixer fitted with the dough hook. Sprinkle the yeast over the contents, drop the butter into the middle of the mixture, and mix on medium to low speed, gradually putting in the powdered milk and sugar. Slowly add in the water and mix until the dough comes away from the bowl, in 5–10 minutes.

2. Remove the dough from the mixing bowl, and set it on the counter to rest for 10 minutes. Return it to the bowl and place on the mixer so the dough hook plunges into the middle of the dough. Mix on medium speed until the dough is soft and pliable, about 15–20 minutes, or until the dough passes the windowpane test. (See page 45.)

3. Remove the dough from the mixing bowl to the counter and gather it up in your hands in a rough ball. Bring the full length of your thumbs into the center of the ball so that they meet, and stretch the dough from the center out, as if opening a book, into an oblong shape. Turn the dough a quarter turn and stretch the dough again the same way, creating a smooth ball. Transfer the

dough to a large mixing bowl, cover it with plastic wrap or a damp kitchen towel, and set it aside in a draft-free place at room temperature until the dough doubles in size, about 45 minutes.

4. Gently remove the dough from the bowl and place it on a clean surface. Cut the dough into 2 pieces (about 1 pound each) and shape them into 2 smooth balls again, as you did before the first rise. Find a surface in your kitchen free from drafts and lay a kitchen towel dusted with flour on it. Place the balls on the towel and cover with plastic wrap or a damp towel to prevent a

Sweet *Fougasse*

This is especially nice for breakfast or for a snack with a cup of tea.

1. After you cut the dough into 2 balls in Step 4, roll each in granulated sugar before you set them aside to proof.

2. Sprinkle a few tablespoons of sugar on the dough before you fold it in half.

crust from forming on the surface. Leave the loaves to proof at room temperature until they double in size, in 20–25 minutes.

5. Preheat the oven to 425°F. Shape the *fougasse* by first patting down the balls to allow the carbonic gasses that have developed to disperse. Pat down the dough and shape it into a rough 4-by-10-inch rectangle. Spread the desired filling (see page 83) down the length of ½ of the dough, leaving a ½-inch rim around the edge. The other half of the dough should be bare. Score this half using the tip of a sharp razor

blade, making 4–6 diagonal slashes along its length. This will be the top of the bread. Fold the scored half over the filled half and seal the dough together with your hands, tucking it underneath itself as you go.

6. Carefully place the loaves on a baking sheet. Brush the tops with the beaten egg using a pastry brush. Sprinkle the sesame seeds or sugar evenly on top, if using. Just before you are ready to slide the baking sheet into the oven, spray the inside of the oven with water using a spray bottle or plant mister and close the door immediately. This will create steam, which promotes a good crust. Put the bread in the oven and bake it for 20 minutes. Transfer the *fougasse* to a rack and allow it to cool before slicing.

Suggested Fillings for *Fougasse*

For savory bread, spread 1/4–1/2 cup of one of the following onto the *fougasse* dough:

- Olive spread (tapenade)
- Tomato sauce with 1/4-inch-thick slices of chorizo or another spicy sausage
- Creamed mushrooms
- Creamed anchovies
- Diced garlic and parsley
- Goat cheese
- Roquefort and crushed walnuts

"To allow your bread to get dirty is to lose a year of your life."

Bread and Wine

Deciding which wine to drink with which bread might seem, to most of us, merely a matter of reaching for the nearest bottle and the nearest loaf. This would be a mistake, as the following tasting notes, compiled by wine experts Joy V. Land and Joseph Uris, show. There is no recommendation for the traditional *baguette, boule,* or *bâtard* because every wine is suitable with them.

The wines provided range from the affordable and easily found to the rarer and more extravagant bottles. Vintages have been omitted to avoid confusing those readers not thoroughly familiar with the dizzying array of wines now available.

The Web site www.wine-searcher.com provides the names of wine stores all over the country where these wines should be available. The more obscure wines have been avoided so all readers will have the opportunity to savor the breads with appropriate wines.

The wines are also available on the Internet through www.sherry-lehmann.com.

Thyme Bread

Sancerre Blanc
Savennières
Châteauneuf-du-Pape Rouge

Pumpkin Bread

Côtes du Ventoux Rouge
St. Joseph Rouge
Minervois Rouge

Apricot and Hazelnut Bread

Muscat de Beaumes-de-Venise
Sauternes
Condrieu

Roquefort Bread

Five- to ten-year-old Tawny Port
Vosne-Romanée or Pommard
Sauternes

Garlic Bread

Rosé de Provence
Gassac Rouge
Bandol Rouge

Walnut and Red Wine Bread

Bergerac Rouge
Madiran
Champagne Rosé

Onion and White Wine Bread

Côtes-du-Ventoux or Roussillon Rouge
Châteauneuf-du-Pape Blanc
Condrieu or Crozes-Hermitage Blanc

Winemaker's Bread

Chilled dry Sherry
Côtes-du-Ventoux Blanc
Muscat de Beaumes-de-Venise

Bacon Bread

By itself:	Crozes-Hermitage
With cassoulet:	Cornas or Cahors
With choucroute:	Pinot Gris d'Alsace
With soup:	Corbières Rouge

Green and Black Olive Bread

Côtes-du-Rhône Villages Rouge
Cahors
Côte-Rôtie

Fisherman's Bread

Tavel Rosé
Châteauneuf-du-Pape Blanc
Hermitage Blanc

Milk Bread

For breakfast:	Black coffee and Armagnac
As lunch sandwiches:	Côtes-du-Rhône, red or white
With butter and chocolate:	Banyuls

Ladder Bread

If sweet:	Sparkling or non-sparkling Vouvray Bandol Rosé
If savory:	Côtes-du-Rhône Blanc Crémant de Bourgogne

Acknowledgments

Authors seldom provide all the ingredients that go into their books, and this is no exception.

Kathleen Hackett, a one-woman *boulangerie,* did a meticulous and invaluable job in the kitchen—testing the recipes, then baking and tasting.

Joy V. Land and Joseph Uris, whose stamina with a corkscrew is admirable, opened countless bottles in search of the ideal wines to accompany each recipe.

In Provence, Ailie Collins organized the mixture of flour and words provided by Gerard Auzet and myself, and helped turn the elements into a manuscript.

And my long-suffering editor, Jon Segal, added several vital pinches of improvement to the text.

To all of you, *un très grand merci.*

—Peter Mayle

A NOTE ON THE TYPE

PIERRE SIMON FOURNIER *le jeune,* who designed the type used in this book, was both an originator and a collector of types. His services to the art of printing were his design of letters, his creation of ornaments and initials, and his standardization of type sizes. His types are old style in character and sharply cut. In 1764 and 1766 he published his *Manuel typographique,* a treatise on the history of French types and printing, on typefounding in all its details, and on what many consider his most important contribution to typography—the measurement of type by the point system.

Composed by North Market Street Graphics,
Lancaster, Pennsylvania
Printed and bound by Rose Printing,
Tallahassee, Florida
Illustrations by Lee Wells
Designed by Virginia Tan